I've Got My Ticket!

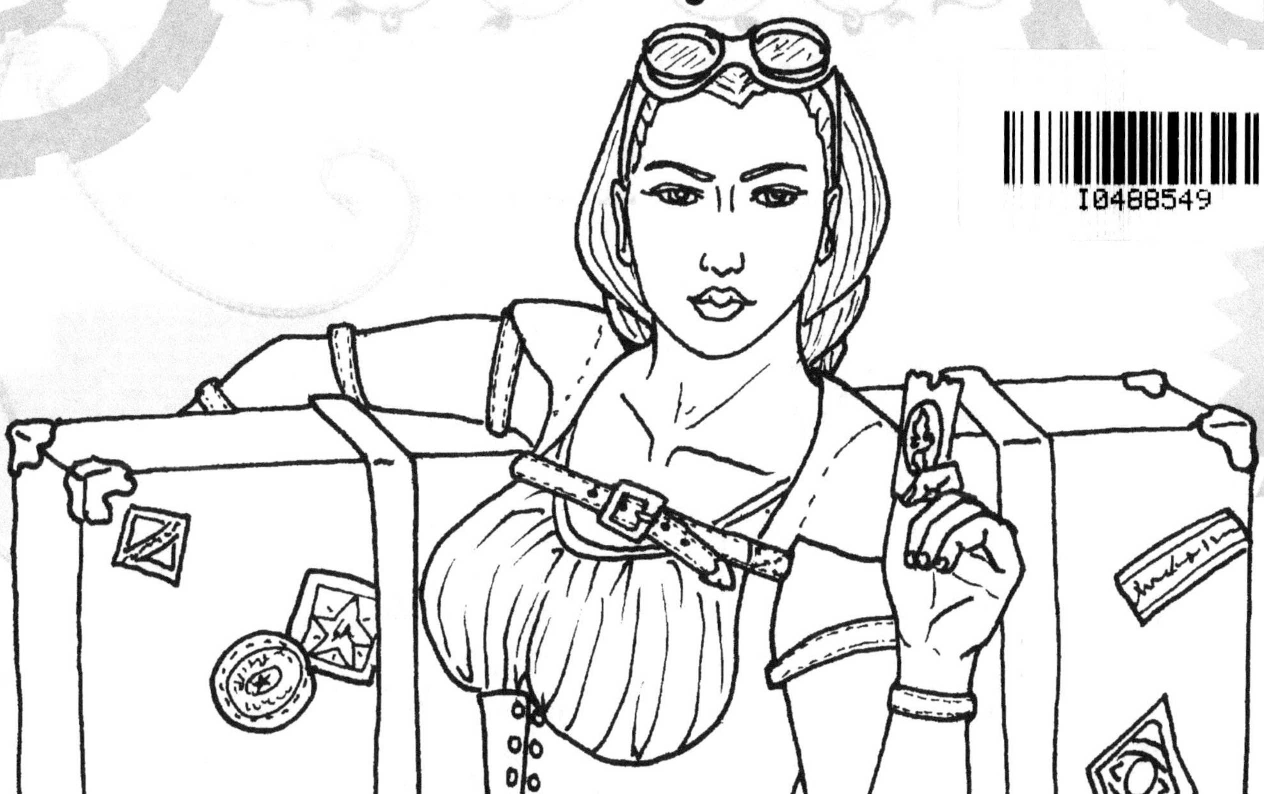

Miss Minerva's
Steampunk Coloring Book

Written and Drawn by
Bobbie Berendson W.

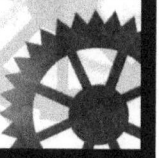

Our Lady of the Gears

Saint Augustine, a city of wonders. One of the most famous sites to visit in beautiful St. Augustine, is the cathedral of the Lady of the Gears.

Built by the talented masons and engineers who call this city home, the cathedral towers over all in St. Augustine. The most stunning part of the cathedral is its massive rose window depicting the patron saint of tinkerers, creative types, and watchmakers. Many a visitor has been awed by the colorful glow that fills the chapel as the sunlight hits the window as it sets for the evening.

It is a fitting tradition that adventurers of all types begin their new endeavors and quests with a visit to this magnificent place of peace and contemplation. Be sure to stop by at sunset when the choir is practicing and the window is shining.

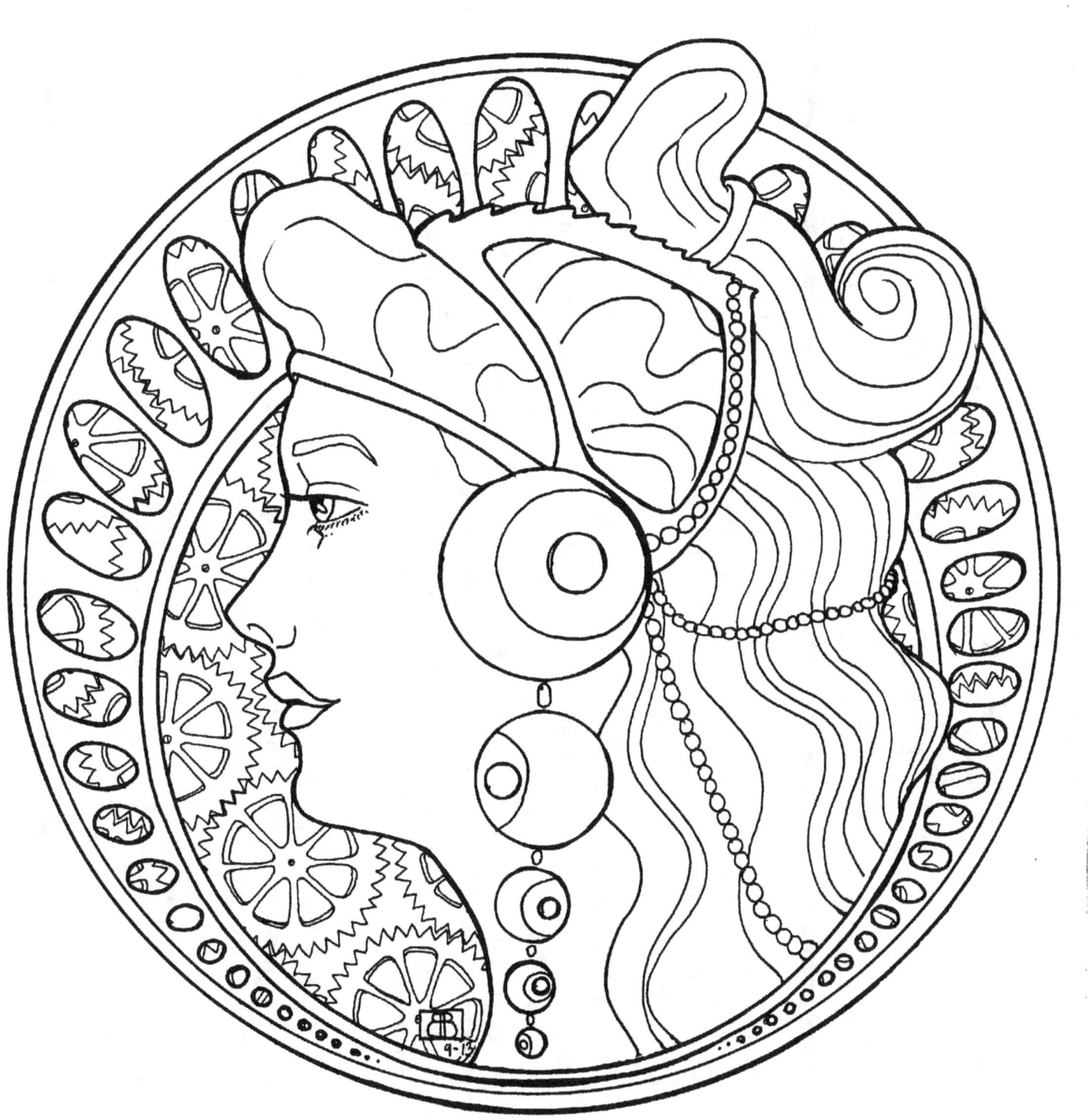

Landon Steele and his Adventuring Guild

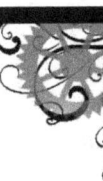

Adventurers young and old have always called the port city of St. Augustine home, but the best known of them has to be Landon Steele and his adventuring guild. Mister Steele comes from an old industrial family and has used his wealth in recent years to foster the adventuring spirit in the youth of the city.

His current group of associate adventurers includes the following members. Ms. Ellie Dale who was top of her class at Herrington Engineering Academy and recruited in the midst of her apprenticeship by Mr. Steele. Col. Dawson, formerly of His Majesties 3rd mechanized infantry and an old college friend of Landon. Ms. Rina Garamond was forced to retire from the ballet stage after a ridding accident, but Mr. Steele offered her a position as a cultural attaché. Mrs. Kathryn Cross is the companies book-keeper and chronicler of their adventures. Pip and his dog Scratch are the most recent additions, having joined the group after an amusing incident involving the Colonel's watch.

Mr. Steele has long shared his belief with others that adventure can be found by anyone of any age. Members of his guild can often be found herding groups of children about town in any of his numerous 'Adventure Day Camps for Kids' projects.

"Anyone can seek out wonder and adventure, all you have to do is take that first step out of your door, open your eyes, Take a deep breath, and jump in."
~(quote from Landon Steele's speech- 'An Adventure a Day')

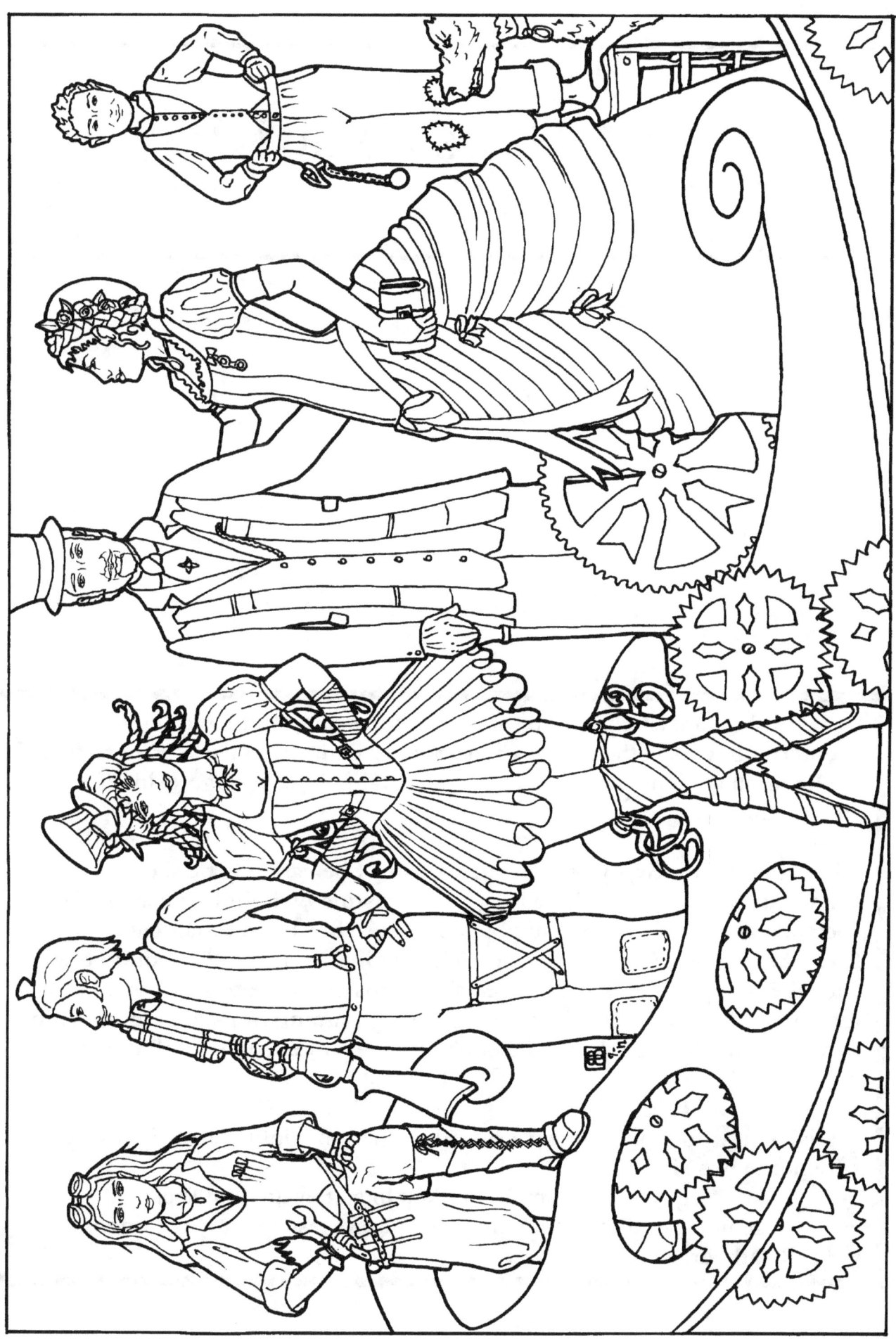

Fire Gypsy Mariska

Another fantastic place to find adventures and affordable entertainments is the Grand Circle Square Pedestrian Park. Entertainers are lined up at all hours of the day to entertain old & young, resident & visitor alike.

'Mariska the Fire Gypsy' is a crowd favorite. She can only be seen in the square as the sun sets and the long St. Augustine twilight begins. Her act is spectacular not only for her acrobatic abilities, but for her magical use of fire. She begins her act by drawing a large circle in red chalk around the spot she is going to perform. Then she warns everyone to stay outside of the circle. Then the lightshow begins, using flaming rings, a flaming whip, and her trained pet goyling* she enchants the audience for a full thirty minutes.

Mariska only does one show per evening when the light is just right. Be sure not to miss it.

        *A goyling is a small monkey-like creature that flies and resembles nothing as much as the gargoyles of many continental cathedrals.

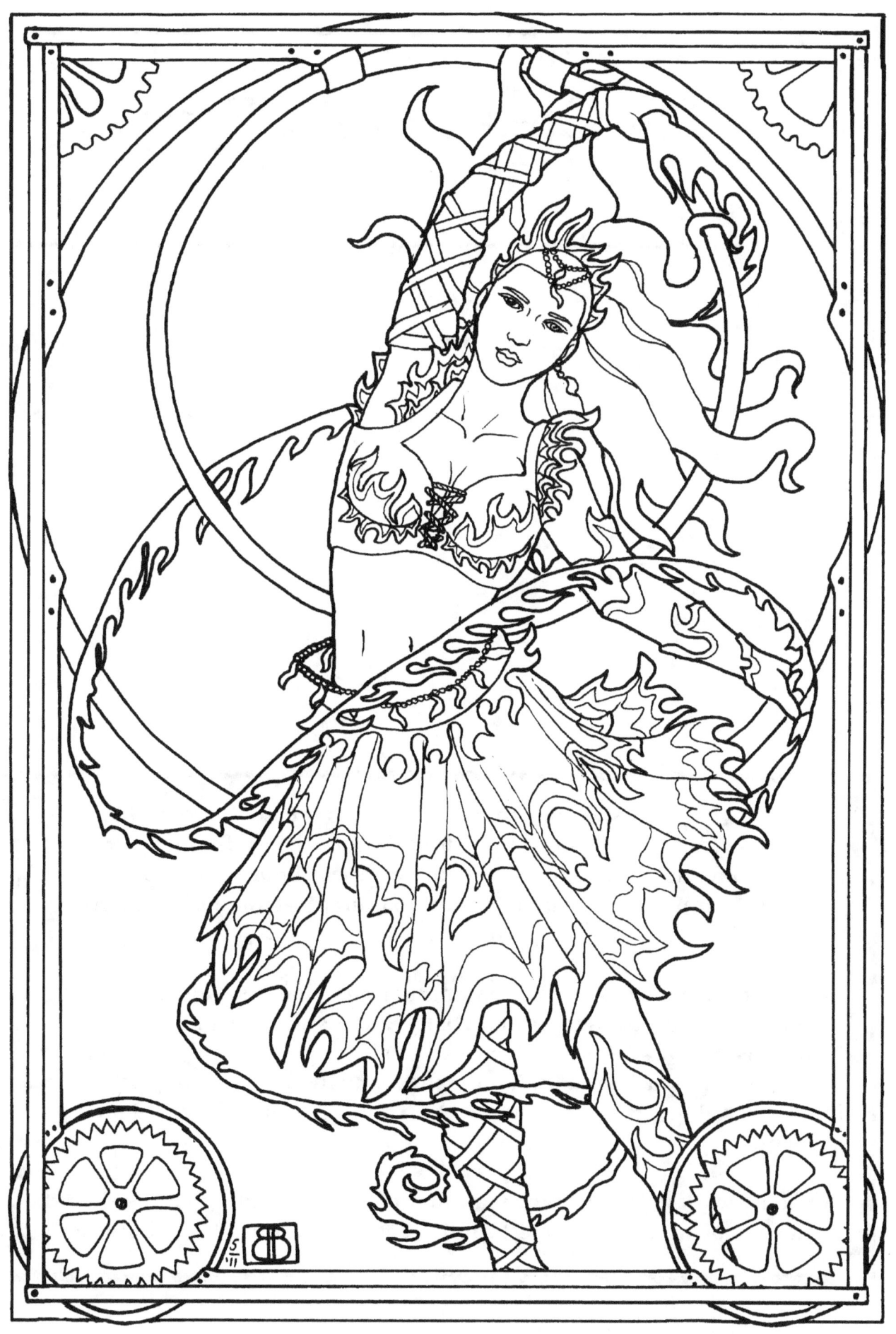

The Steampunk Fairy

St. Augustine is well known for it's curious theater district. Just about any kind of theater can be found, from the traditionally dramatic to modern comedic. There are also plenty of opera houses and ballet parlors. An up and coming new trend is a combination of acrobatics, dancing, music, and media.

Here we have St. Augustine's Steampunk Fairy, one Ms. Adeline Stephenson. Trained in traditional ballet and dance, she has taken the theater district by storm by directing and starring in a number of her own 'Steampunk Flights of Fancy". Her shows include such daring exploits as tightrope walking, trapeze artists, ribbon dancers, musicians, balancing acts, and more.

Her latest work tells the whimsical story of how geared up fairies keep the town clock running properly and the trials and travails of doing so.

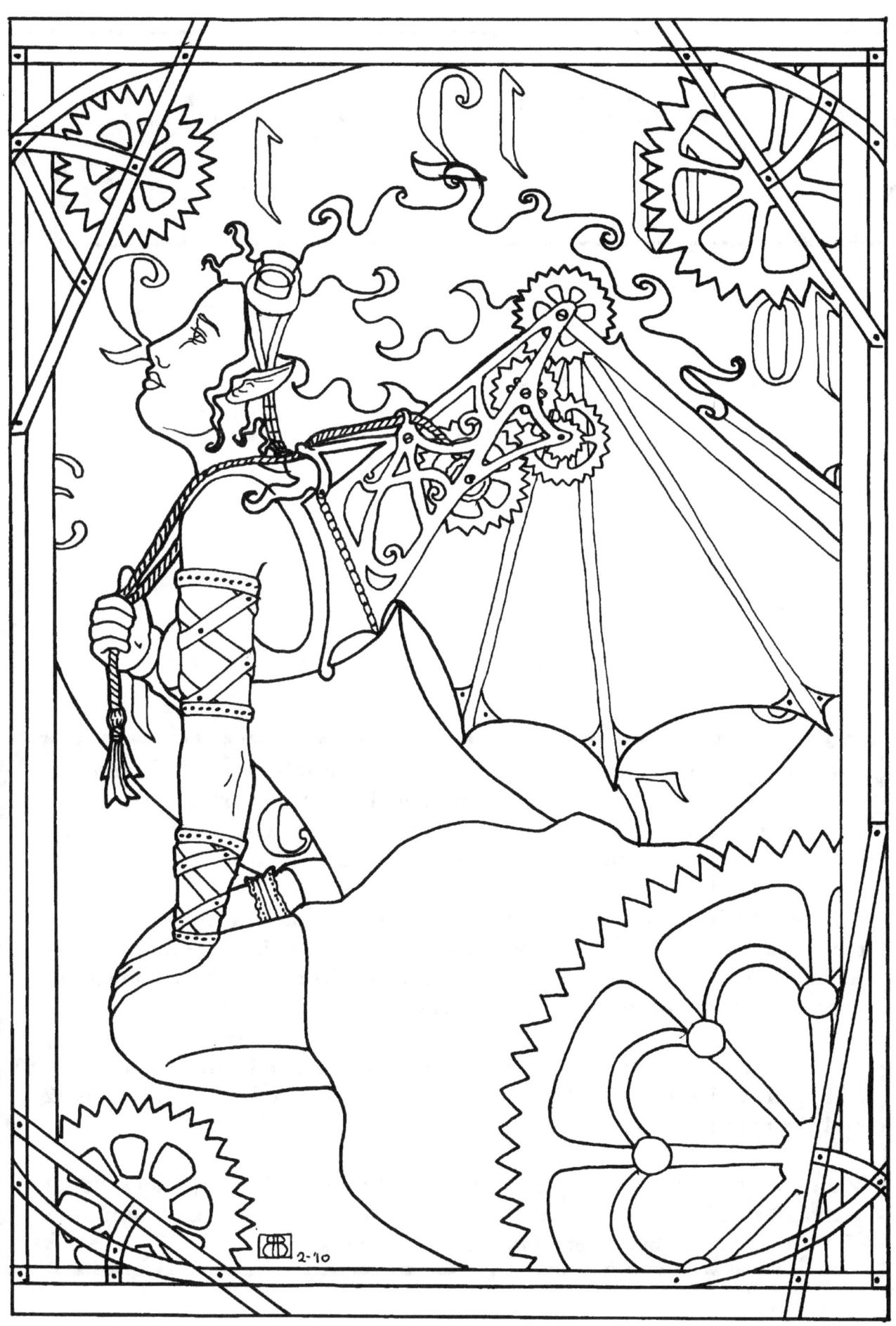

Ralph Jr. & the Girls

Rarely does a single man of such gifted gear minded genius come along as St' Augustine's own Ralph Bricklesbury. Ralph is a true metal minded man and though he is now retired the city has been gifted with his children who seemed to inherit his gear-mindedness.

The Bricklesbury clan, also referred to as simply 'Ralph's Girls' even though the youngest is a boy, have made their way into the public eye many times. As builders, bustle racers, mechanics, and engineers, they have shown the entire city that your mind is what maters.

The clan roster is as follows top to bottom: Alexia age 16, the Twins: Elizabeth & Ellenor ages 17, Lydia age 13, Rafina age 18, Ralph Jr. age 12 and Claire age 14.

Though very close in friendship, the girls admittedly do have many friendly rivalries with each other. While Jr. writes very interesting and humorous novels about his sisters and their adventures.

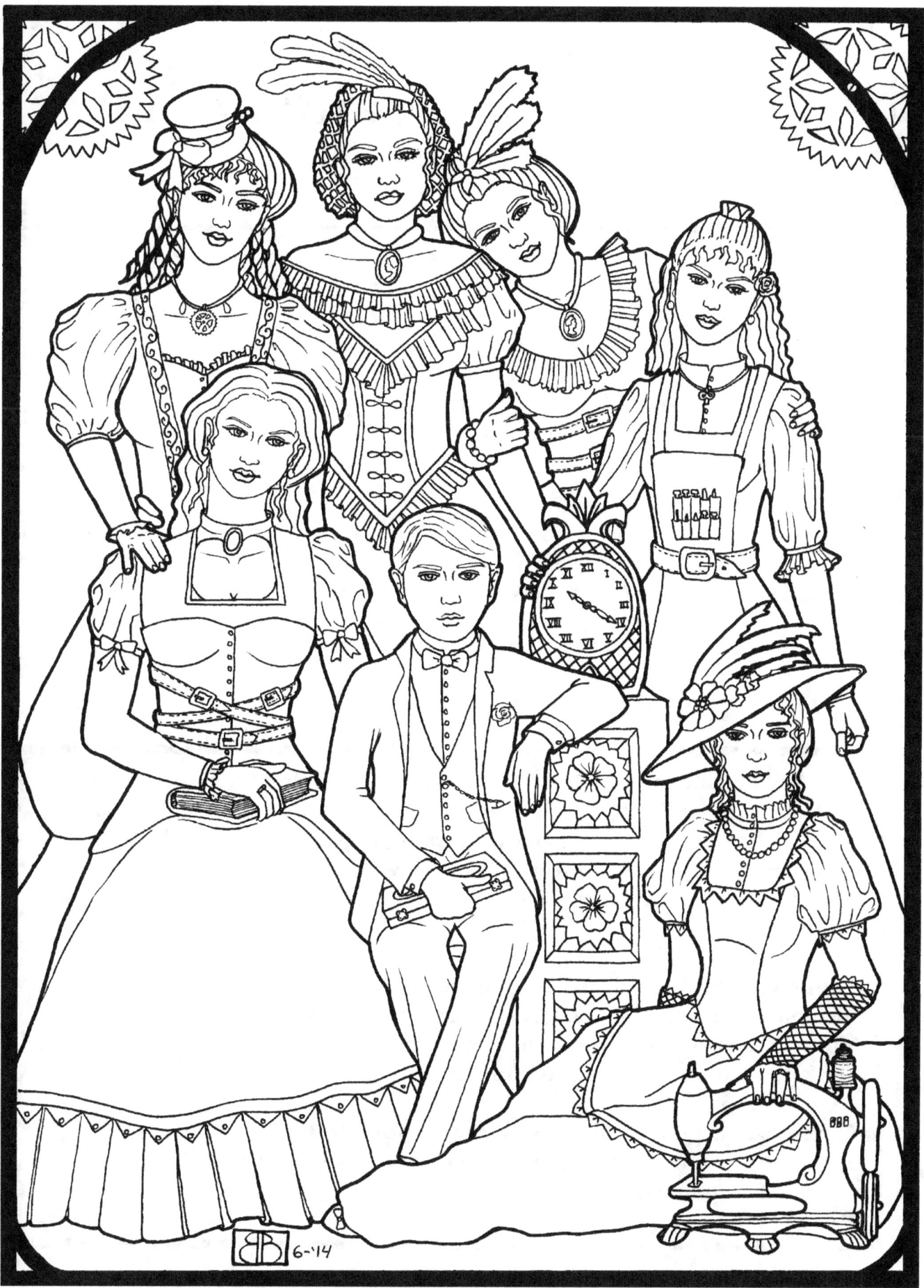

Alexia at Work and at Play

A life balancing work and play can be challenging for some, not for Alexia Bricklesbury, fourth daughter of the famed mechanic known as Ralph. She begins her days elbow deep in grease and cogs working on one of her many ingenious devices, has lunch with the boys on her crew, then heads home to clean up and dress for whatever socialite occasion she has for the evening.

Though possibly not the prettiest of Ralph's girls, Alexia is the most sociable and a very popular guest at any upper class event. She is often found at these parties entertaining a large group of metal-minded men like her father with tales of life and limb among the gears.

Alexia has recently founded a charitable organization to benefit the widows of the brave men who work the engines of our ships, trains, Dirigibles, and flying machines.

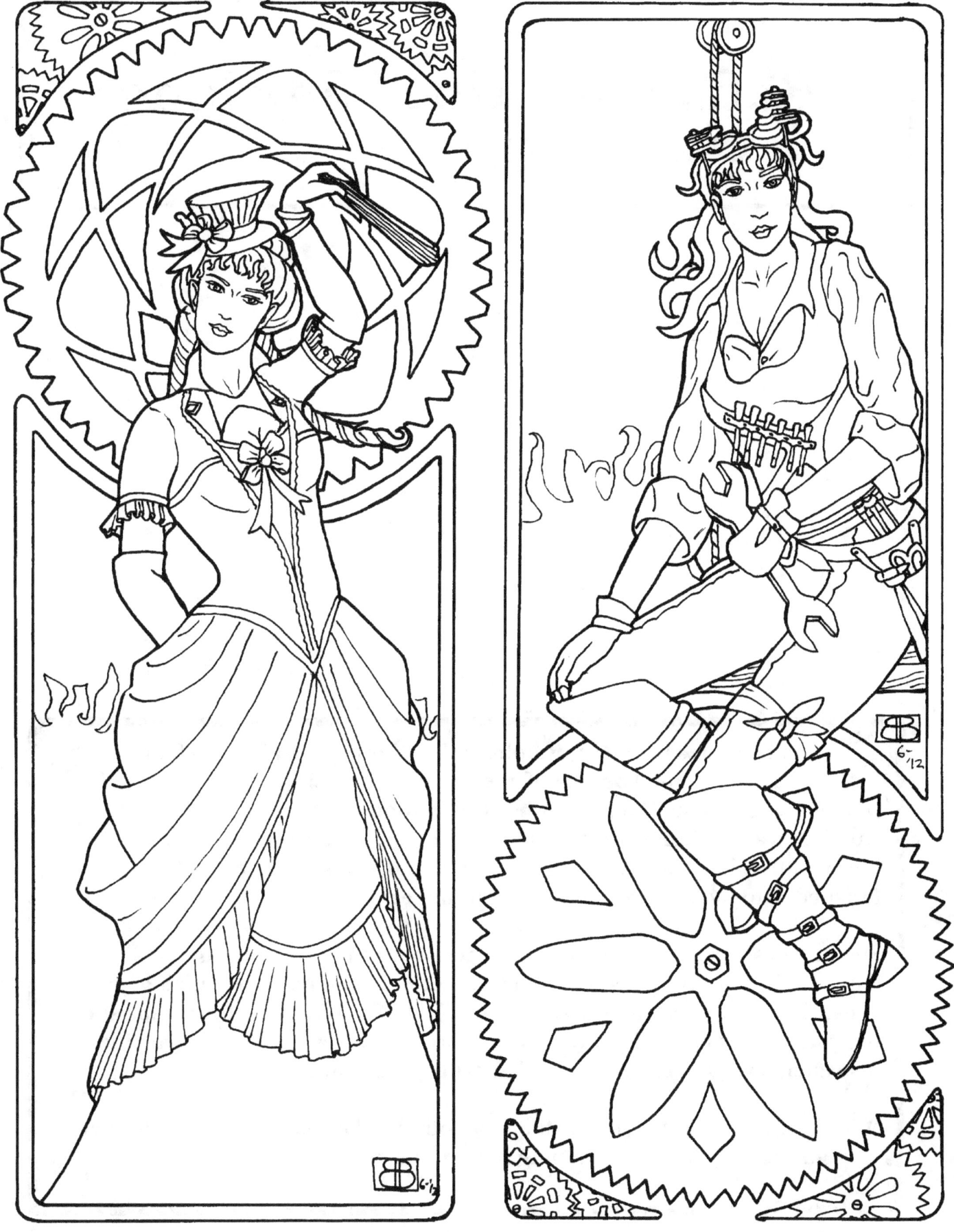

Rafina in Striped Stockings

An adventuress at heart, Ralph's eldest daughter Rafina prefers to ply her trade abroad on one of the several flying ships she has helped pioneer. Early in her life, her father Ralph took her to work with him often while he was working with a close group of engineers on a new flying ship. Her youthful ideas and drawings inspired and amused the engineers and the finished ship looked strongly similar to her art.

She began saving money then to buy her own ship and at the age of 19, with a little help from Ralph, she purchased her first. Full of enterprising spirit she quickly grew her budding company, Wild Winds, to the four ships she has today. Her company offers local tourist flights around St. Augustine and it's waterways, as well as long and short trips abroad.

While travelling, Rafina can usually be found either on deck sketching her guests or below deck helping her engineers.

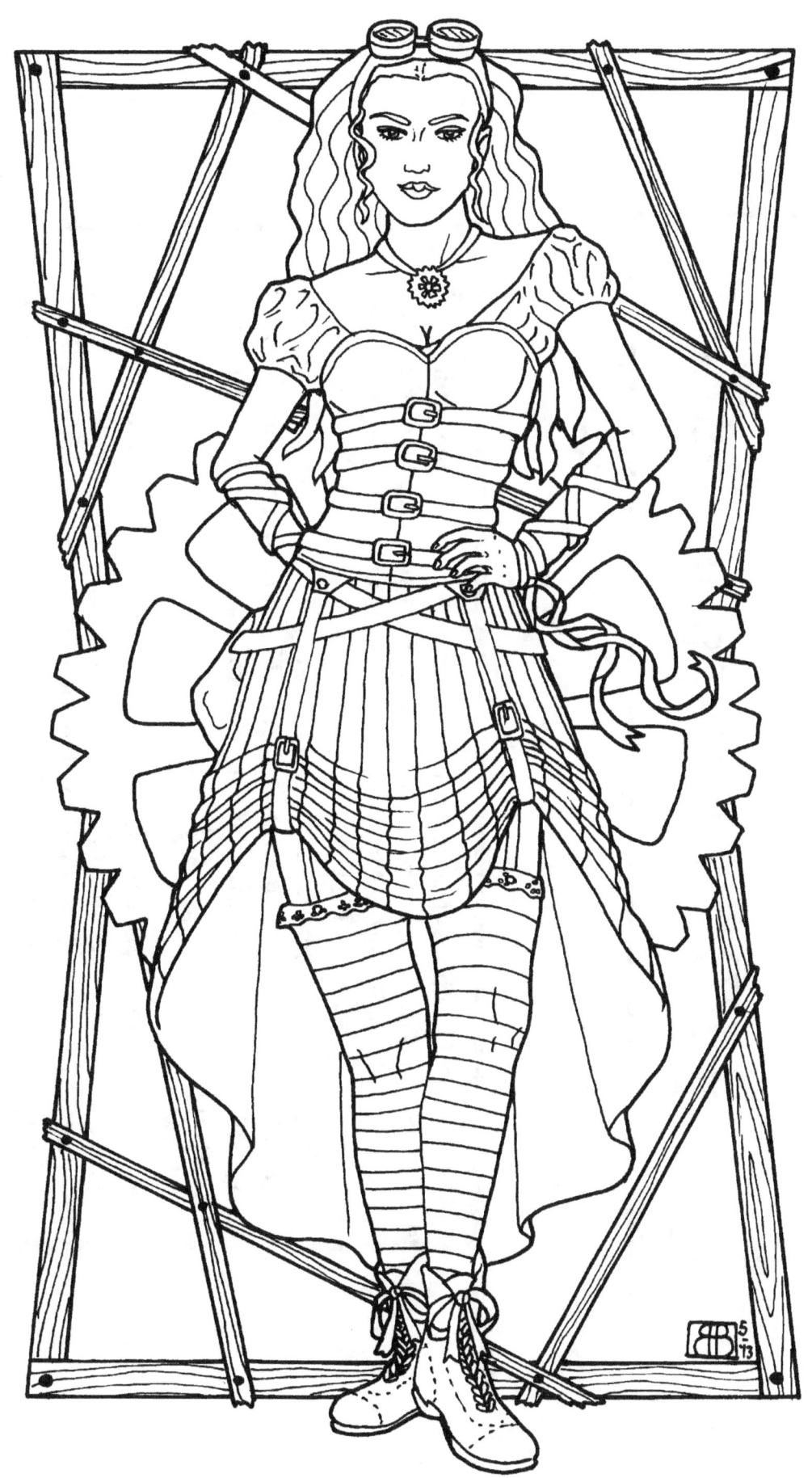

A Treat After the Skytour
at EB's Confectionarium

Not all of Ralph's girls build huge machines or budding empires. The Second daughter Elizabeth, specializes in smaller machines that make sugary confections. Also called the 'Sweets Queen' of St. Augustine, Elizabeth began by intently watching her mother in the kitchen. Every time her father brought home a gizmo or gadget to help her mother's work load in the kitchen she would fine tune them and keep them running. It wasn't long before she was making plans for new machines that chilled cream or pulled sugar.

Today she runs a very special sweets shop in St. Augustine along the bustling boardwalk overlooking the boat harbor and airship port. The city's favorite treats are available there such as, lemon ice, berry custard, almond cranberry cookies, toasted nuts, salt water taffy, and more. You can even watch Elizabeth and the machines at work through the large workshop windows.

Be sure to visit after your flying tour of the city.

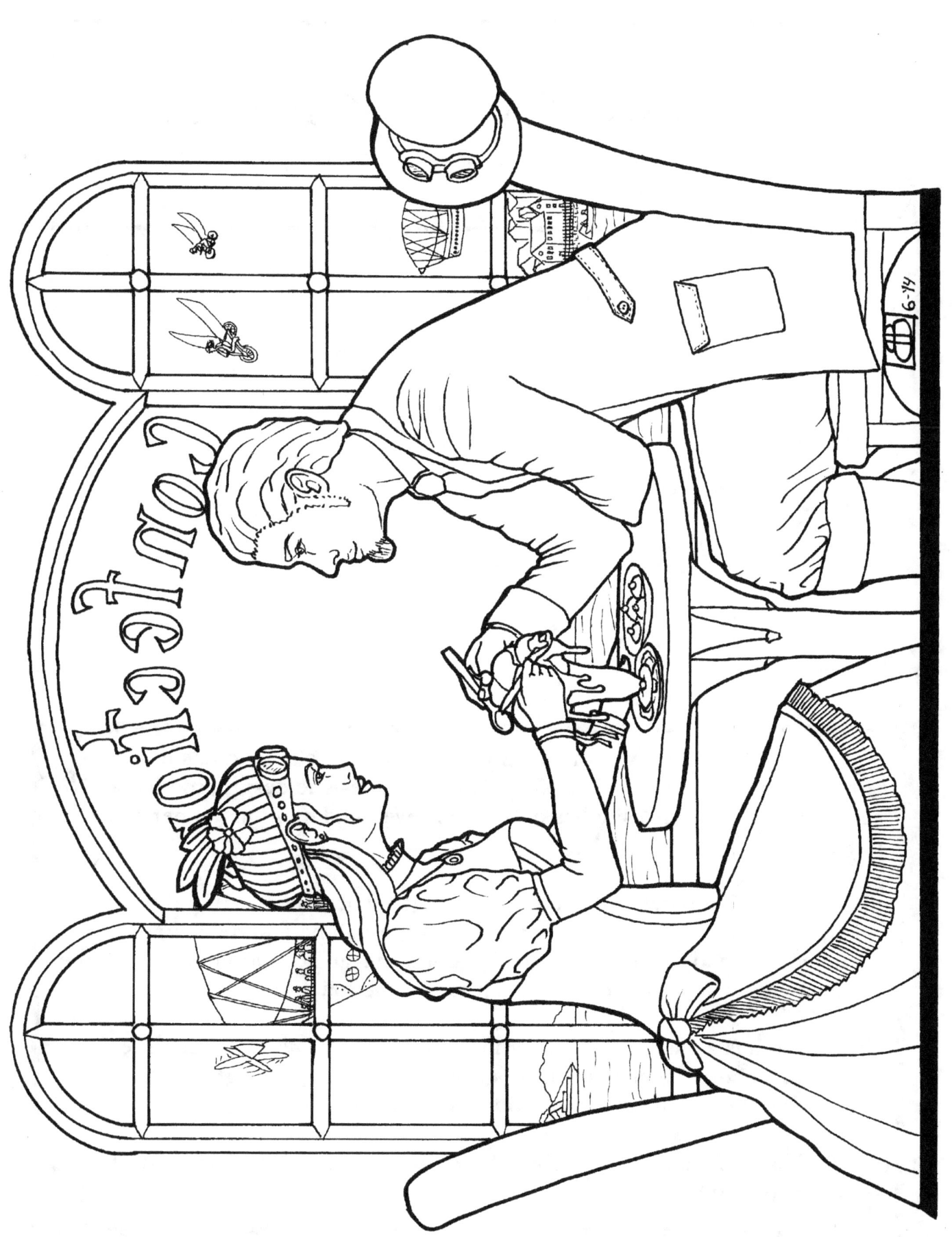

Claire the Couturiere

Claire Bricklesbury is the third youngest of the clan and has found her place in the fashion industry. Not only does she design, model, and sew her own creations, she has developed several adaptations to her sewing machine.

She won her first patent on one of her designs when she was 16. It was an ingenious device that attached to any sewing machine and mechanically gathered fabric to make ruffles. Her second was an addition to the machine pedals to make it smoother and easier to run the machine.

Claire also has a passion for Haberdashery and is always sketching ideas for simple to elaborate hats. She makes use of her custom designed ribbons and laces not only on her dresses but also her hats.

With many a famous client, Claire hopes to someday design an outfit for the queen herself.

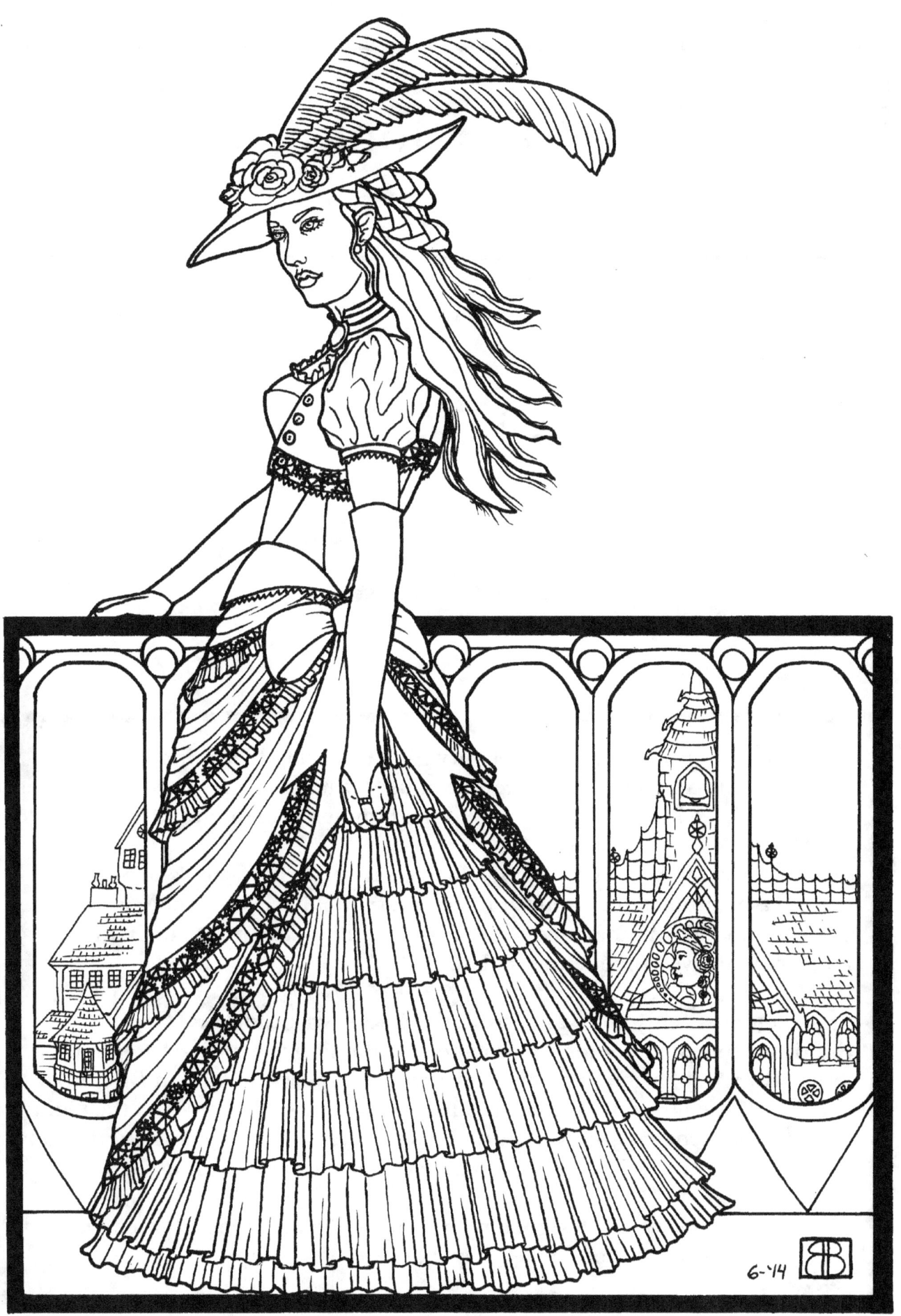

Lydia the Clock Queen

The youngest of the Bricklesbury girls is Lydia. Her mind is a maze of ticking gears and careful timing. Even as a baby she loved clocks and often fell asleep curled up next to the families ancient grandfather clock.

Lydia completed her first working clock with her father when she was just 14. It was a simple affair housed in an amateurishly carved wooden case made to look like a pineapple. She was and still is very proud of it and it keeps perfect even time ten years later.

At the age of twenty she was recruited to the town's Clocker's Guild. The Guild is responsible for tending to and maintaining the cities more than three dozen public clocks as well as the most important clock in Brickman Square. The enormous Brickman Square clock, or Old Cranky as the Guild calls it, has become Lydia's favorite. It was always a touchy clock with many quirks, but under Lydia's maintenance it has never been more accurate.

In her working leathers designed by her sister Claire, she is a force to be reckoned with if you are a faulty clock.

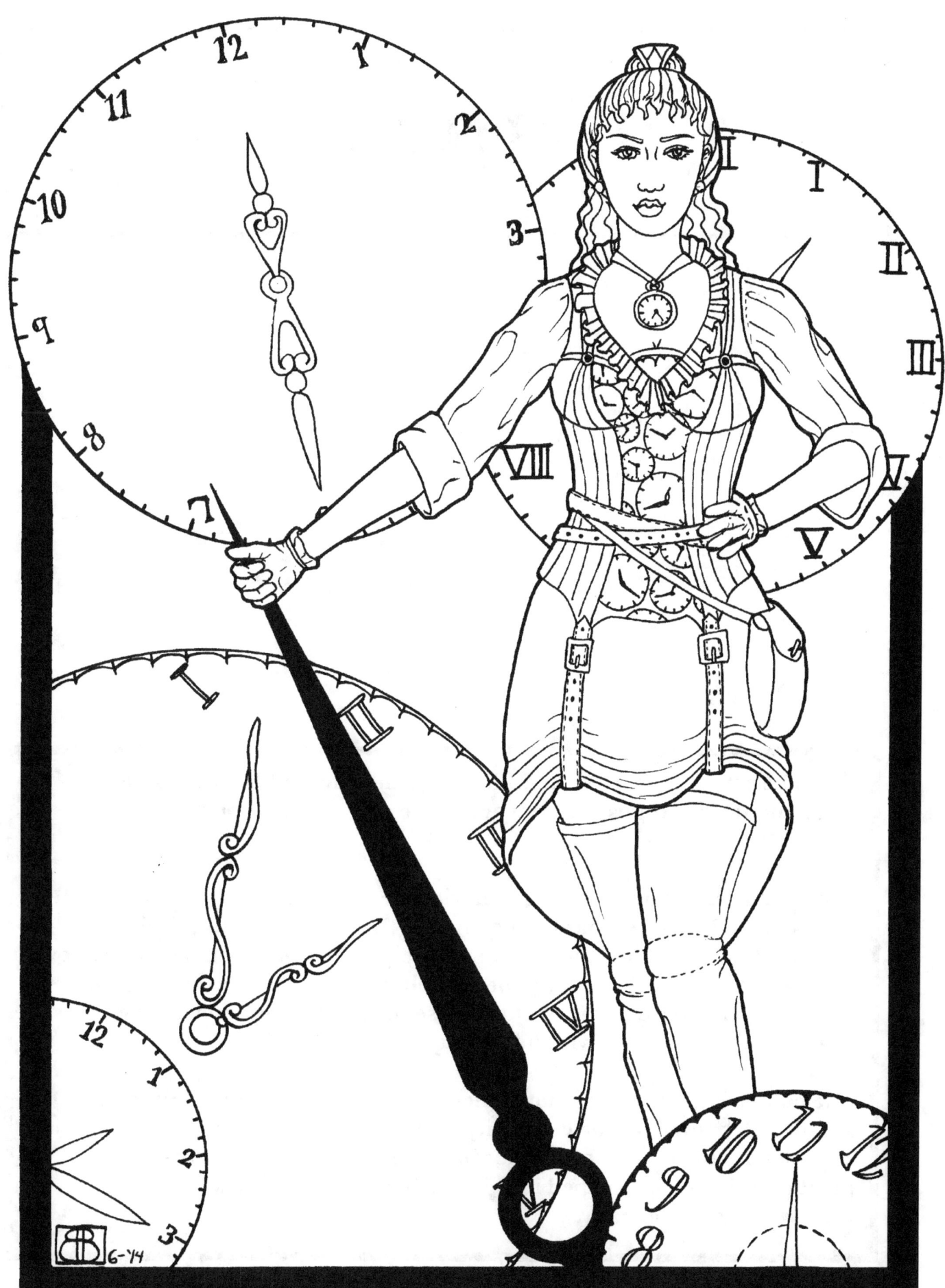

Stuck

The artistic duo of Veoma Littleston and Richard Durrant have been taking the St. Augustine art world by storm with their photo-graphy series "Beauty in the Machine."

Veoma is a well known artist model with the amazing ability to hold a pose precisely for hours. Richard is a genius in the field of photo-graphy. Shortly after their initial meeting at a gallery opening, they began to work together on creative ideas for photo-graphic imagery. It wasn't long after that they announced to the world their series of photo-graphy of the beautiful Veoma posing with machinery and gears.

The couple has since announced their engagement and are planning an artistic celebration for the entire city to participate in instead of a reception. The plan is still a secret but rumor has it that there will be fireworks, a parade, and lollipops shaped like gears. The whole city is anxiously waiting for the party.

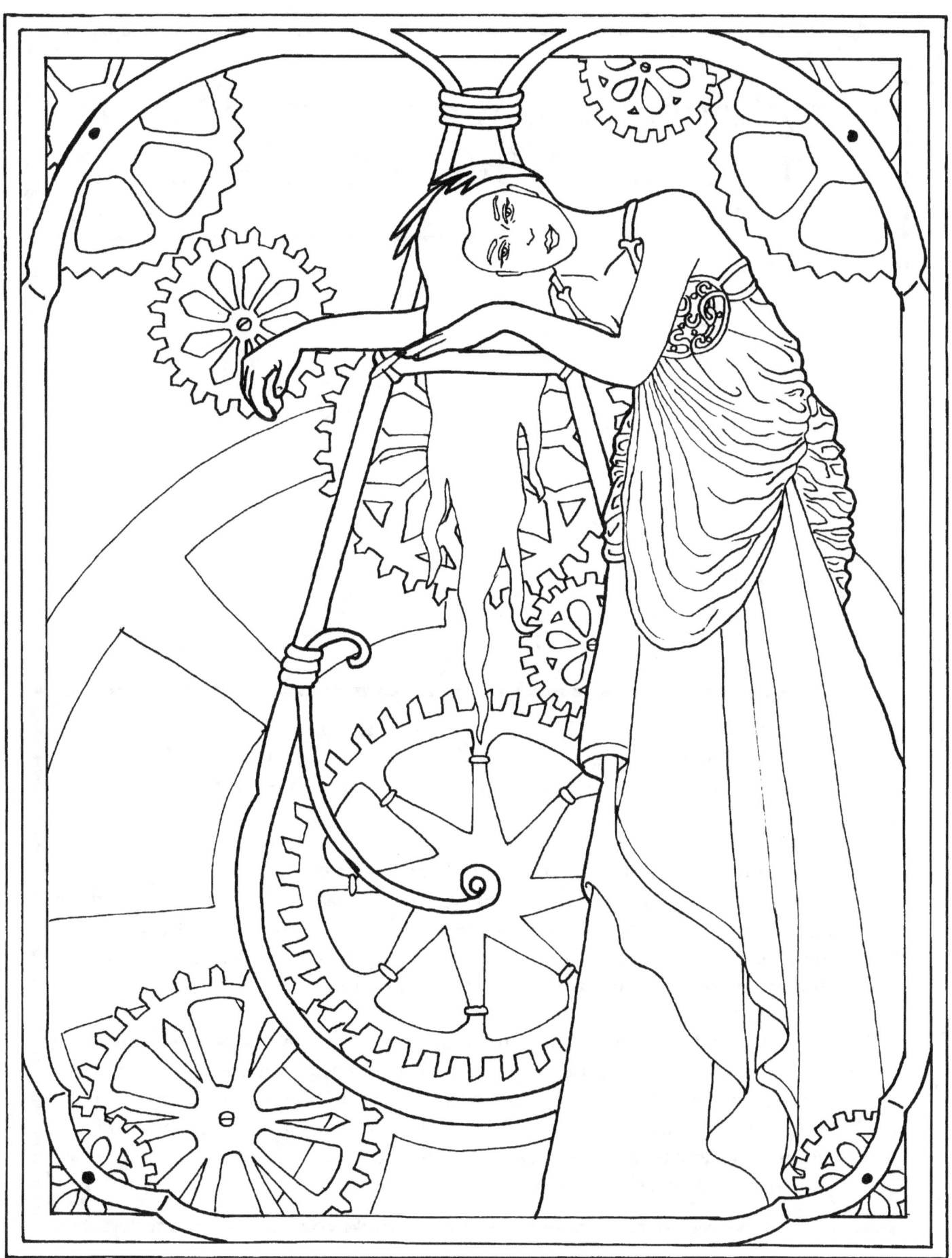

Lady Lenore & Gnome Gustavus of the St. Augustine Bustle Racing Club

A favorite sport in St. Augustine is racing, airship racing, horse racing, and Bustle racing. Young and old, high and low born alike line the boardwalks on Saturday afternoons to watch the pageant that is the bustle races.

Each race consists of six to ten racers. Each racer consists of one gnomish pilot, one generally high born woman who is the 'face' of the racer, and their spring powered rig. The gnome keeps the rig going and steers, the lady is counterbalance and poise. Since the races are equal parts race and pageant the role of the 'face' is just as important as the pilot.

Though usually low speed and genteel, small tussles do occasionally break out around corners where the judges lose sight of the contestants. The ladies will try to disturb each other's posture, ruffle hair, smudge make-up, rattle nerves, or force one another to drop items. All these factors are judged and scored. One can win the race time wise and still lose if the 'face' is not pristine and perfectly polished.

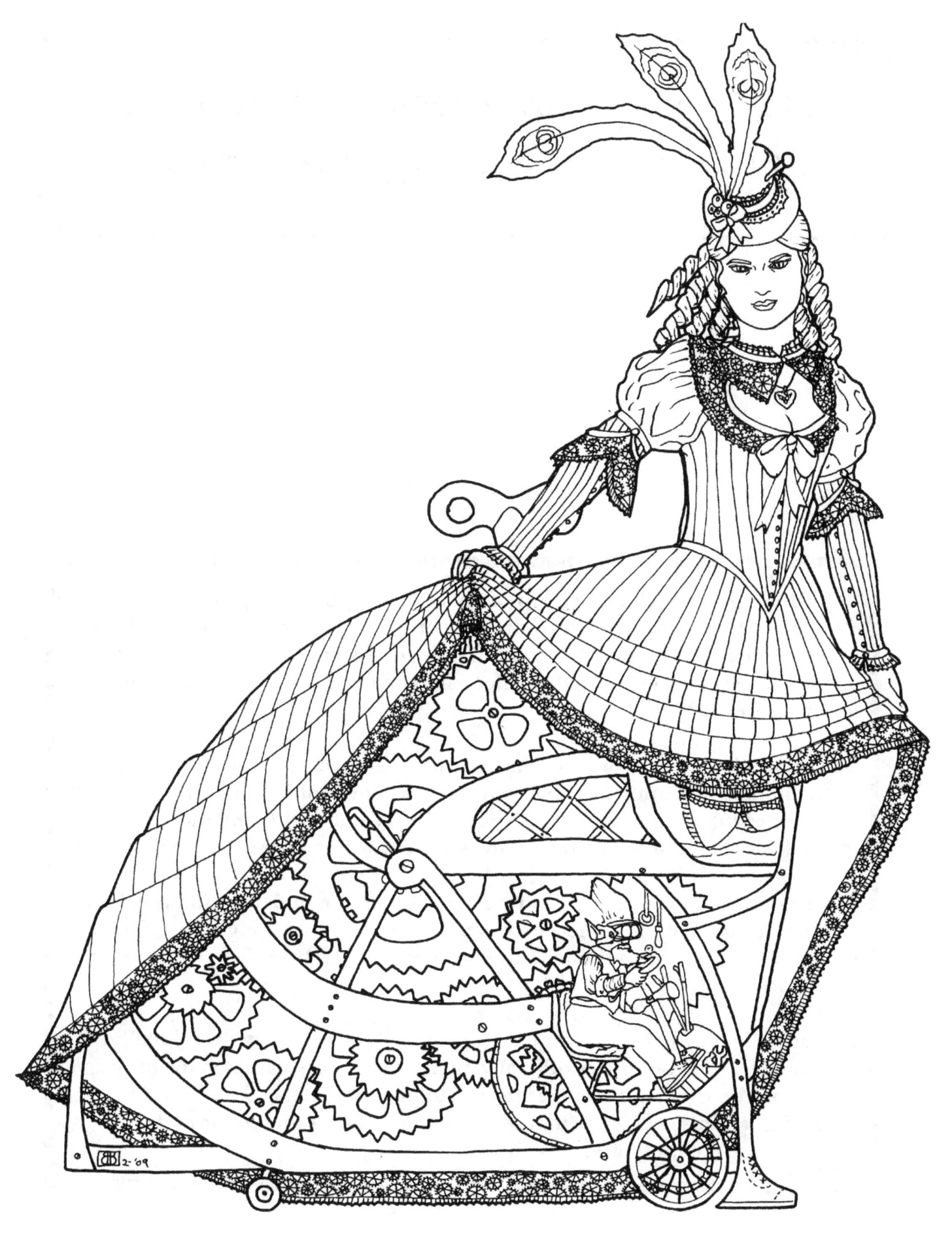

Ellenor and Gnomess Grinda of the DeLancey St. Underground Racers

Although the genteel version of this sport is primarily practiced on the public boardwalks, the more adventurous version is to be found underground on the old city streets. The streets were covered over a century ago and have since been used as cheep housing and are the prime locations for shady dealings.

Once a week the corridors are cleared out for the races. Ladies not of high birth are most common as racers but the occasional high born lady has been seen underground racing. The tunnels are very hot during the races and most of the girls prefer to do the racing in as little clothing as is safe.

The biggest differences from above racers is that the underground bustles are steam powered therefore they are much faster and more dangerous. So are the underground racers though, and bruises and black eyes are common in this sport.

It is also the only place that female gnomes will be seen outside of the home. Not allowed to pilot bustles officially, many a gnomess with an adventuring spirit find their way to the underground to become pilots. Some bustle racing enthusiasts insist that they are better pilots than their male Gnome counterparts.

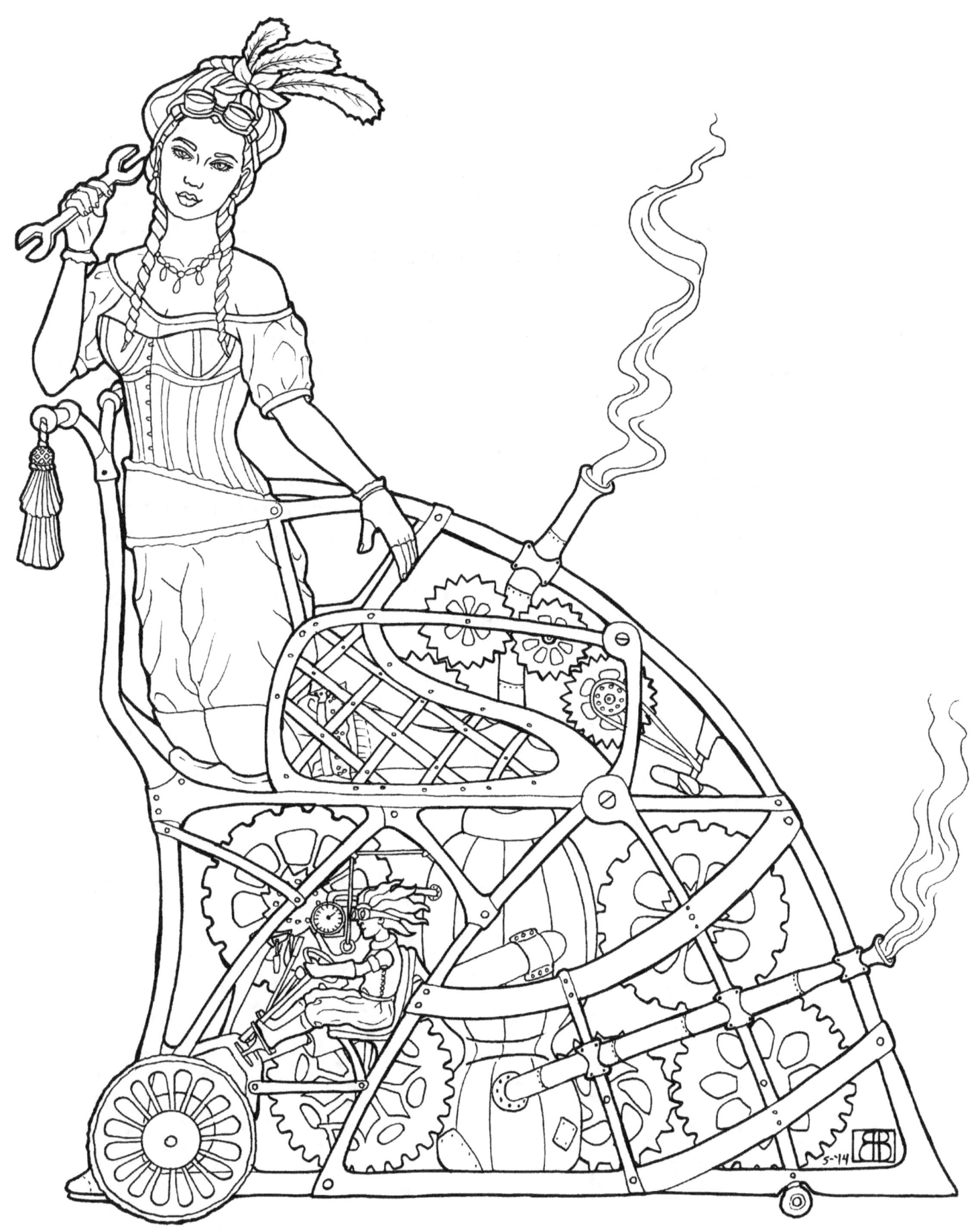

Why Steampunk?

I love the Steampunk Aesthetic. I have always loved anything gear-ish, mechanically whimsical, and Victorian. Not sure why, but I do. Here are some more awesome places to learn the basic definitions and see more of this epic creative cultural phenomena:

http://en.wikipedia.org/wiki/Steampunk
http://www.steampunk.com/what-is-steampunk/
http://www.pbs.org/arts/exhibit/off-book-episode-4-steampunk/

Thanks!
Thanks to all my family and friends, especially my hubby, for many hours worth of time discussing the finer points and rules of Bustle Racing and it's participants. Thanks to my husband Steve, the kids Tim and Alex, and my sisters Tami and Amberly for helping me with ideas, construction, and distribution of these works. And thanks to my sister Sara who has given me the courage to get out in public and sell my art and curios.

Bobbie Berendson W.

www.ingramcontent.com/pod-product-compliance
Lightning Source LLC
Chambersburg PA
CBHW081315170526
45166CB00011B/3536